MW00885170

Eat Great Food

_____

_____

_____

 Table of Contents

Page #	Recipe Name	Type	Date

 Table of Contents

Page #	Recipe Name	Type	Date

Recipe Name:

_____

_____

Date: _____

Type: _____

Difficulty: 1 2 3 4 5 6 7 8 9 10

Serves:
_____

Prep Time:
_____

Cook Time:
_____

Oven Temp:
_____

Notes:
_____
_____
_____
_____
_____

Ingredients:

_____
_____
_____
_____
_____
_____
_____
_____
_____
_____
_____

Directions:

_____
_____
_____
_____
_____
_____
_____
_____
_____
_____
_____

Directions continued:

_____
_____
_____
_____
_____
_____
_____
_____
_____
_____
_____

Photos & Notes:

Recipe Name:

_____

_____

Date: _____

Type: _____

Difficulty: 1 2 3 4 5 6 7 8 9 10

Serves:

_____

Prep Time:

_____

Cook Time:

_____

Oven Temp:

_____

Notes:

_____

_____

_____

_____

_____

Ingredients:

_____

_____

_____

_____

_____

_____

_____

_____

_____

_____

_____

_____

_____

Directions:

_____

_____

_____

_____

_____

_____

_____

_____

_____

_____

_____

_____

Directions continued:

_____
_____
_____
_____
_____
_____
_____
_____
_____
_____
_____
_____

Photos & Notes:

Recipe Name:

_____

_____

Date: _____

Type: _____

Difficulty: 1 2 3 4 5 6 7 8 9 10

Serves:

_____

Prep Time:

_____

Cook Time:

_____

Oven Temp:

_____

Notes:

_____

_____

_____

_____

_____

Ingredients:

_____

_____

_____

_____

_____

_____

_____

_____

_____

_____

_____

Directions:

_____

_____

_____

_____

_____

_____

_____

_____

_____

_____

Directions continued:

Photos & Notes:

Recipe Name:

_____

_____

Date: _____

Type: _____

Difficulty: 1 2 3 4 5 6 7 8 9 10

Serves:

_____

Prep Time:

_____

Cook Time:

_____

Oven Temp:

_____

Notes:

_____

_____

_____

_____

_____

Ingredients:

_____

_____

_____

_____

_____

_____

_____

_____

_____

_____

Directions:

_____

_____

_____

_____

_____

_____

_____

_____

_____

_____

_____

13

Directions continued:

_____
_____
_____
_____
_____
_____
_____
_____
_____
_____
_____
_____
_____

Photos & Notes:

Recipe Name:
_____
_____

Date: _____

Type: _____

Difficulty: 1 2 3 4 5 6 7 8 9 10

Serves:
_____

Prep Time:
_____

Cook Time:
_____

Oven Temp:
_____

Notes:
_____
_____
_____
_____
_____

Ingredients:

_____
_____
_____
_____
_____
_____
_____
_____
_____
_____
_____
_____
_____
_____

Directions:

_____
_____
_____
_____
_____
_____
_____
_____
_____
_____
_____
_____
_____
_____

Directions continued:

_____
_____
_____
_____
_____
_____
_____
_____
_____
_____
_____
_____

Photos & Notes:

Recipe Name:
_____
_____

Date: _____
Type: _____
Difficulty: 1 2 3 4 5 6 7 8 9 10

Serves:
_____

Prep Time:
_____

Cook Time:
_____

Oven Temp:
_____

Notes:
_____
_____
_____
_____
_____

Ingredients:
_____
_____
_____
_____
_____
_____
_____
_____
_____
_____

Directions:
_____
_____
_____
_____
_____
_____
_____
_____
_____

Directions continued:

_____
_____
_____
_____
_____
_____
_____
_____
_____
_____
_____
_____

Photos & Notes:

Recipe Name:

Date: _____

Type: _____

Difficulty: 1 2 3 4 5 6 7 8 9 10

Serves:

_____

Prep Time:

_____

Cook Time:

_____

Oven Temp:

_____

Notes:

_____
_____
_____
_____
_____

Ingredients:

_____
_____
_____
_____
_____
_____
_____
_____
_____
_____
_____

Directions:

_____
_____
_____
_____
_____
_____
_____
_____
_____
_____
_____

Directions continued:

_____
_____
_____
_____
_____
_____
_____
_____
_____
_____
_____
_____
_____

Photos & Notes:

Recipe Name:

_____

_____

Date: _____

Type: _____

Difficulty: 1 2 3 4 5 6 7 8 9 10

Serves:

_____

Prep Time:

_____

Cook Time:

_____

Oven Temp:

_____

Notes:

_____

_____

_____

_____

_____

Ingredients:

_____
_____
_____
_____
_____
_____
_____
_____
_____
_____
_____
_____

Directions:

_____
_____
_____
_____
_____
_____
_____
_____
_____
_____
_____
_____

Directions continued:

Photos & Notes:

Recipe Name:
_____
_____

Date: _____
Type: _____
Difficulty: 1 2 3 4 5 6 7 8 9 10

Serves:
_____

Prep Time:
_____

Cook Time:
_____

Oven Temp:
_____

Notes:
_____
_____
_____
_____
_____

Ingredients:
_____
_____
_____
_____
_____
_____
_____
_____
_____
_____
_____

Directions:
_____
_____
_____
_____
_____
_____
_____
_____
_____
_____
_____

23

Directions continued:

_____
_____
_____
_____
_____
_____
_____
_____
_____
_____
_____

Photos & Notes:

Recipe Name:

_____

_____

Date: _____

Type: _____

Difficulty: 1 2 3 4 5 6 7 8 9 10

Serves:

_____

Prep Time:

_____

Cook Time:

_____

Oven Temp:

_____

Notes:

_____

_____

_____

_____

_____

_____

Ingredients:

_____

_____

_____

_____

_____

_____

_____

_____

_____

_____

_____

Directions:

_____

_____

_____

_____

_____

_____

_____

_____

_____

_____

_____

25

Directions continued:

_____
_____
_____
_____
_____
_____
_____
_____
_____
_____
_____
_____
_____

Photos & Notes:

Recipe Name:
_____
_____

Date: _____
Type: _____
Difficulty: 1 2 3 4 5 6 7 8 9 10

Serves:
_____

Prep Time:
_____

Cook Time:
_____

Oven Temp:
_____

Notes:
_____
_____
_____
_____
_____
_____

Ingredients:
_____
_____
_____
_____
_____
_____
_____
_____
_____
_____

Directions:
_____
_____
_____
_____
_____
_____
_____
_____
_____
_____

Directions continued:

_____
_____
_____
_____
_____
_____
_____
_____
_____
_____
_____
_____

Photos & Notes:

Recipe Name:

_____

_____

Date: _____

Type: _____

Difficulty: 1 2 3 4 5 6 7 8 9 10

Serves:

_____

Prep Time:

_____

Cook Time:

_____

Oven Temp:

_____

Notes:

_____

_____

_____

_____

_____

Ingredients:

_____
_____
_____
_____
_____
_____
_____
_____
_____
_____

Directions:

_____
_____
_____
_____
_____
_____
_____
_____
_____
_____

Directions continued:

_____
_____
_____
_____
_____
_____
_____
_____
_____
_____
_____
_____
_____

Photos & Notes:

Recipe Name:

_____

_____

Date: _____

Type: _____

Difficulty: 1 2 3 4 5 6 7 8 9 10

Serves:

_____

Prep Time:

_____

Cook Time:

_____

Oven Temp:

_____

Notes:

_____

_____

_____

_____

_____

Ingredients:

_____

_____

_____

_____

_____

_____

_____

_____

_____

_____

Directions:

_____

_____

_____

_____

_____

_____

_____

_____

_____

_____

Directions continued:

_____
_____
_____
_____
_____
_____
_____
_____
_____
_____
_____

Photos & Notes:

Recipe Name:

_____

_____

Date: _____

Type: _____

Difficulty: 1 2 3 4 5 6 7 8 9 10

Serves:

_____

Prep Time:

_____

Cook Time:

_____

Oven Temp:

_____

Notes:

_____

_____

_____

_____

_____

_____

Ingredients:

_____
_____
_____
_____
_____
_____
_____
_____
_____
_____
_____

Directions:

_____
_____
_____
_____
_____
_____
_____
_____
_____
_____
_____

Directions continued:

Photos & Notes:

Recipe Name:
_____
_____

Date: _____
Type: _____
Difficulty: 1 2 3 4 5 6 7 8 9 10

Serves:
_____

Prep Time:
_____

Cook Time:
_____

Oven Temp:
_____

Notes:
_____
_____
_____
_____
_____

Ingredients:
_____
_____
_____
_____
_____
_____
_____
_____
_____
_____
_____

Directions:
_____
_____
_____
_____
_____
_____
_____
_____
_____
_____
_____

Directions continued:

_____

_____

_____

_____

_____

_____

_____

_____

_____

_____

_____

_____

Photos & Notes:

Recipe Name:

_____

_____

Date: _____

Type: _____

Difficulty: 1 2 3 4 5 6 7 8 9 10

Serves:

_____

Prep Time:

_____

Cook Time:

_____

Oven Temp:

_____

Notes:

_____

_____

_____

_____

_____

Ingredients:

_____

_____

_____

_____

_____

_____

_____

_____

_____

_____

_____

_____

Directions:

_____

_____

_____

_____

_____

_____

_____

_____

_____

_____

_____

_____

Directions continued:

_____
_____
_____
_____
_____
_____
_____
_____
_____
_____
_____

Photos & Notes:

Recipe Name:

_____

_____

Date: _____

Type: _____

Difficulty: 1 2 3 4 5 6 7 8 9 10

Serves:

_____

Prep Time:

_____

Cook Time:

_____

Oven Temp:

_____

Notes:

_____

_____

_____

_____

_____

Ingredients:

_____

_____

_____

_____

_____

_____

_____

_____

_____

_____

_____

_____

Directions:

_____

_____

_____

_____

_____

_____

_____

_____

_____

_____

_____

_____

Directions continued:

_____
_____
_____
_____
_____
_____
_____
_____
_____
_____
_____

Photos & Notes:

Recipe Name:

_____

_____

Date: _____

Type: _____

Difficulty: 1 2 3 4 5 6 7 8 9 10

Serves:

_____

Prep Time:

_____

Cook Time:

_____

Oven Temp:

_____

Notes:

_____

_____

_____

_____

_____

Ingredients:

_____

_____

_____

_____

_____

_____

_____

_____

_____

_____

Directions:

_____

_____

_____

_____

_____

_____

_____

_____

_____

_____

41

Directions continued:

_____
_____
_____
_____
_____
_____
_____
_____
_____
_____
_____

Photos & Notes:

Recipe Name:

_____
_____

Date: _____

Type: _____

Difficulty: 1 2 3 4 5 6 7 8 9 10

Serves:

_____

Prep Time:

_____

Cook Time:

_____

Oven Temp:

_____

Notes:

_____
_____
_____
_____
_____
_____

Ingredients:

_____
_____
_____
_____
_____
_____
_____
_____
_____
_____

Directions:

_____
_____
_____
_____
_____
_____
_____
_____
_____
_____

Directions continued:

_____
_____
_____
_____
_____
_____
_____
_____
_____
_____
_____
_____

Photos & Notes:

Recipe Name:
_____
_____

Date: _____
Type: _____
Difficulty: 1 2 3 4 5 6 7 8 9 10

Serves:
_____

Prep Time:
_____

Cook Time:
_____

Oven Temp:
_____

Notes:
_____
_____
_____
_____
_____

Ingredients:
_____
_____
_____
_____
_____
_____
_____
_____
_____
_____
_____

Directions:
_____
_____
_____
_____
_____
_____
_____
_____
_____
_____

Directions continued:

_____
_____
_____
_____
_____
_____
_____
_____
_____
_____
_____

Photos & Notes:

Recipe Name:
_____
_____

Date: _____

Type: _____

Difficulty: 1 2 3 4 5 6 7 8 9 10

Serves:
_____

Prep Time:
_____

Cook Time:
_____

Oven Temp:
_____

Notes:
_____
_____
_____
_____
_____

Ingredients:
_____
_____
_____
_____
_____
_____
_____
_____
_____
_____

Directions:
_____
_____
_____
_____
_____
_____
_____
_____
_____

Directions continued:

_____
_____
_____
_____
_____
_____
_____
_____
_____
_____
_____

Photos & Notes:

Recipe Name:

_____

_____

Date: _____

Type: _____

Difficulty: 1 2 3 4 5 6 7 8 9 10

Serves:

_____

Prep Time:

_____

Cook Time:

_____

Oven Temp:

_____

Notes:

_____

_____

_____

_____

_____

Ingredients:

_____
_____
_____
_____
_____
_____
_____
_____
_____
_____
_____

Directions:

_____
_____
_____
_____
_____
_____
_____
_____
_____
_____

49

Directions continued:

_____
_____
_____
_____
_____
_____
_____
_____
_____
_____
_____
_____
_____
_____

Photos & Notes:

Recipe Name:

_____

_____

Date: _____

Type: _____

Difficulty: 1 2 3 4 5 6 7 8 9 10

Serves:

_____

Prep Time:

_____

Cook Time:

_____

Oven Temp:

_____

Notes:

_____

_____

_____

_____

_____

Ingredients:

Directions:

_____

_____

_____

_____

_____

_____

_____

_____

_____

_____

Directions continued:

_____
_____
_____
_____
_____
_____
_____
_____
_____
_____
_____

Photos & Notes:

Recipe Name:
_____
_____

Date: _____

Type: _____

Difficulty: 1 2 3 4 5 6 7 8 9 10

Serves:
_____

Prep Time:
_____

Cook Time:
_____

Oven Temp:
_____

Notes:
_____
_____
_____
_____
_____

Ingredients:

Directions:

53

Directions continued:

_____

_____

_____

_____

_____

_____

_____

_____

_____

_____

_____

Photos & Notes:

Recipe Name:
_____
_____

Date: _____
Type: _____
Difficulty: 1 2 3 4 5 6 7 8 9 10

Serves:
_____
Prep Time:
_____

Cook Time:
_____
Oven Temp:
_____

Notes:
_____
_____
_____
_____
_____
_____

Ingredients:
_____
_____
_____
_____
_____
_____
_____
_____
_____
_____
_____
_____
_____

Directions:
_____
_____
_____
_____
_____
_____
_____
_____
_____
_____
_____
_____

Directions continued:

Photos & Notes:

Recipe Name:
_____
_____

Date: _____
Type: _____
Difficulty: 1 2 3 4 5 6 7 8 9 10

Serves:
_____

Prep Time:
_____

Cook Time:
_____

Oven Temp:
_____

Notes:
_____
_____
_____
_____
_____

Ingredients:

_____
_____
_____
_____
_____
_____
_____
_____
_____
_____
_____
_____

Directions:

_____
_____
_____
_____
_____
_____
_____
_____
_____
_____
_____
_____

Directions continued:

_____

_____

_____

_____

_____

_____

_____

_____

_____

_____

_____

_____

Photos & Notes:

Recipe Name:

_____

_____

Date: _____

Type: _____

Difficulty: 1 2 3 4 5 6 7 8 9 10

Serves:	Cook Time:
_____	_____
Prep Time:	Oven Temp:
_____	_____

Notes:

_____

_____

_____

_____

_____

Ingredients:

_____
_____
_____
_____
_____
_____
_____
_____
_____
_____
_____
_____

Directions:

_____
_____
_____
_____
_____
_____
_____
_____
_____
_____
_____
_____

Directions continued:

Photos & Notes:

Recipe Name:

_____
_____

Date: _____

Type: _____

Difficulty: 1 2 3 4 5 6 7 8 9 10

Serves:

_____

Prep Time:

_____

Cook Time:

_____

Oven Temp:

_____

Notes:

_____
_____
_____
_____
_____
_____

Ingredients:

_____
_____
_____
_____
_____
_____
_____
_____
_____
_____

Directions:

_____
_____
_____
_____
_____
_____
_____
_____
_____
_____

Directions continued:

_____
_____
_____
_____
_____
_____
_____
_____
_____
_____
_____
_____
_____

Photos & Notes:

Recipe Name:

_____

_____

Date: _____

Type: _____

Difficulty: 1 2 3 4 5 6 7 8 9 10

Serves:

_____

Prep Time:

_____

Cook Time:

_____

Oven Temp:

_____

Notes:

_____

_____

_____

_____

_____

Ingredients:

_____

_____

_____

_____

_____

_____

_____

_____

_____

_____

_____

Directions:

_____

_____

_____

_____

_____

_____

_____

_____

_____

_____

Directions continued:

_____
_____
_____
_____
_____
_____
_____
_____
_____
_____
_____
_____

Photos & Notes:

Recipe Name:
_____
_____

Date: _____

Type: _____

Difficulty: 1 2 3 4 5 6 7 8 9 10

Serves:
_____

Prep Time:
_____

Cook Time:
_____

Oven Temp:
_____

Notes:
_____
_____
_____
_____
_____
_____

Ingredients:
_____
_____
_____
_____
_____
_____
_____
_____
_____
_____
_____
_____

Directions:
_____
_____
_____
_____
_____
_____
_____
_____
_____
_____
_____

Directions continued:

_____
_____
_____
_____
_____
_____
_____
_____
_____
_____
_____
_____
_____

Photos & Notes:

Recipe Name:

_____

_____

Date: _____

Type: _____

Difficulty: 1 2 3 4 5 6 7 8 9 10

Serves:

_____

Prep Time:

_____

Cook Time:

_____

Oven Temp:

_____

Notes:

_____
_____
_____
_____
_____
_____

Ingredients:

_____
_____
_____
_____
_____
_____
_____
_____
_____
_____
_____
_____

Directions:

_____
_____
_____
_____
_____
_____
_____
_____
_____
_____
_____

Directions continued:

_____
_____
_____
_____
_____
_____
_____
_____
_____
_____
_____
_____
_____

Photos & Notes:

Recipe Name:
_____
_____

Date: _____
Type: _____
Difficulty: 1 2 3 4 5 6 7 8 9 10

Serves:
_____

Prep Time:
_____

Cook Time:
_____

Oven Temp:
_____

Notes:
_____
_____
_____
_____
_____
_____

Ingredients:
_____
_____
_____
_____
_____
_____
_____
_____
_____
_____
_____

Directions:
_____
_____
_____
_____
_____
_____
_____
_____
_____
_____

Directions continued:

_____
_____
_____
_____
_____
_____
_____
_____
_____
_____
_____
_____
_____

Photos & Notes:

Recipe Name:
_____
_____

Date: _____

Type: _____

Difficulty: 1 2 3 4 5 6 7 8 9 10

Serves:
_____

Prep Time:
_____

Cook Time:
_____

Oven Temp:
_____

Notes:
_____
_____
_____
_____
_____
_____

Ingredients:
_____
_____
_____
_____
_____
_____
_____
_____
_____
_____
_____

Directions:
_____
_____
_____
_____
_____
_____
_____
_____
_____
_____
_____

Directions continued:

_____
_____
_____
_____
_____
_____
_____
_____
_____
_____
_____
_____

Photos & Notes:

Recipe Name:

_____

_____

Date: _____

Type: _____

Difficulty: 1 2 3 4 5 6 7 8 9 10

Serves:

_____

Prep Time:

_____

Cook Time:

_____

Oven Temp:

_____

Notes:

_____

_____

_____

_____

_____

Ingredients:

_____
_____
_____
_____
_____
_____
_____
_____
_____
_____

Directions:

_____
_____
_____
_____
_____
_____
_____
_____

Directions continued:

_____
_____
_____
_____
_____
_____
_____
_____
_____
_____
_____
_____

Photos & Notes:

Recipe Name:

_____

_____

Date: _____

Type: _____

Difficulty: 1 2 3 4 5 6 7 8 9 10

Serves:

_____

Prep Time:

_____

Cook Time:

_____

Oven Temp:

_____

Notes:

_____

_____

_____

_____

_____

_____

Ingredients:

_____

_____

_____

_____

_____

_____

_____

_____

_____

_____

_____

Directions:

_____

_____

_____

_____

_____

_____

_____

_____

_____

_____

Directions continued:

_____
_____
_____
_____
_____
_____
_____
_____
_____
_____
_____
_____
_____

Photos & Notes:

Recipe Name:
_____
_____

Date: _____

Type: _____

Difficulty: 1 2 3 4 5 6 7 8 9 10

Serves:
_____

Prep Time:
_____

Cook Time:
_____

Oven Temp:
_____

Notes:
_____
_____
_____
_____
_____
_____

Ingredients:

_____
_____
_____
_____
_____
_____
_____
_____
_____

Directions:

_____
_____
_____
_____
_____
_____
_____
_____
_____

Directions continued:

Photos & Notes:

Recipe Name:

_____
_____

Date: _____
Type: _____
Difficulty: 1 2 3 4 5 6 7 8 9 10

Serves:
_____

Prep Time:
_____

Cook Time:
_____

Oven Temp:
_____

Notes:
_____
_____
_____
_____
_____

Ingredients:

_____
_____
_____
_____
_____
_____
_____
_____
_____
_____
_____

Directions:

_____
_____
_____
_____
_____
_____
_____
_____
_____
_____
_____

Directions continued:

_____
_____
_____
_____
_____
_____
_____
_____
_____
_____
_____
_____
_____

Photos & Notes:

Recipe Name:

_____

_____

Date: _____

Type: _____

Difficulty: 1 2 3 4 5 6 7 8 9 10

Serves:
_____

Prep Time:
_____

Cook Time:
_____

Oven Temp:
_____

Notes:
_____
_____
_____
_____
_____
_____

Ingredients:

_____
_____
_____
_____
_____
_____
_____
_____
_____
_____

Directions:

_____
_____
_____
_____
_____
_____
_____
_____
_____
_____

Directions continued:

_____
_____
_____
_____
_____
_____
_____
_____
_____
_____
_____
_____
_____
_____

Photos & Notes:

Recipe Name:
_____
_____

Date: _____
Type: _____
Difficulty: 1 2 3 4 5 6 7 8 9 10

Serves:
_____

Prep Time:
_____

Cook Time:
_____

Oven Temp:
_____

Notes:
_____
_____
_____
_____
_____
_____

Ingredients:
_____
_____
_____
_____
_____
_____
_____
_____
_____
_____
_____
_____

Directions:
_____
_____
_____
_____
_____
_____
_____
_____
_____
_____
_____

Directions continued:

_____

_____

_____

_____

_____

_____

_____

_____

_____

_____

_____

Photos & Notes:

Recipe Name:

_____
_____

Date: _____
Type: _____
Difficulty: 1 2 3 4 5 6 7 8 9 10

Serves:
_____

Prep Time:
_____

Cook Time:
_____

Oven Temp:

Notes:
_____
_____
_____
_____
_____

Ingredients:

_____
_____
_____
_____
_____
_____
_____
_____
_____
_____

Directions:

_____
_____
_____
_____
_____
_____
_____
_____
_____
_____

Directions continued:

_____
_____
_____
_____
_____
_____
_____
_____
_____
_____
_____

Photos & Notes:

Recipe Name:

_____

_____

Date: _____

Type: _____

Difficulty: 1 2 3 4 5 6 7 8 9 10

Serves:

_____

Prep Time:

_____

Cook Time:

_____

Oven Temp:

Notes:

_____

_____

_____

_____

_____

_____

Ingredients:

_____

_____

_____

_____

_____

_____

_____

_____

_____

_____

Directions:

_____

_____

_____

_____

_____

_____

_____

_____

_____

_____

Directions continued:

_____
_____
_____
_____
_____
_____
_____
_____
_____
_____
_____
_____

Photos & Notes:

Recipe Name:

_____
_____

Date: _____

Type: _____

Difficulty: 1 2 3 4 5 6 7 8 9 10

Serves:

_____

Prep Time:

_____

Cook Time:

_____

Oven Temp:

_____

Notes:

_____
_____
_____
_____
_____

Ingredients:

_____
_____
_____
_____
_____
_____
_____
_____
_____
_____
_____

Directions:

_____
_____
_____
_____
_____
_____
_____
_____
_____

Directions continued:

_____
_____
_____
_____
_____
_____
_____
_____
_____
_____
_____

Photos & Notes:

Recipe Name:

_____

_____

Date: _____

Type: _____

Difficulty: 1 2 3 4 5 6 7 8 9 10

Serves:

_____

Prep Time:

_____

Cook Time:

_____

Oven Temp:

_____

Notes:

_____

_____

_____

_____

_____

Ingredients:

_____
_____
_____
_____
_____
_____
_____
_____
_____
_____
_____
_____
_____
_____

Directions:

_____
_____
_____
_____
_____
_____
_____
_____
_____
_____
_____
_____
_____
_____

Directions continued:

_____
_____
_____
_____
_____
_____
_____
_____
_____
_____
_____

Photos & Notes:

Recipe Name:
_____
_____

Date: _____

Type: _____

Difficulty: 1 2 3 4 5 6 7 8 9 10

Serves:
_____

Prep Time:
_____

Cook Time:
_____

Oven Temp:
_____

Notes:
_____
_____
_____
_____
_____

Ingredients:
_____
_____
_____
_____
_____
_____
_____
_____
_____
_____
_____

Directions:
_____
_____
_____
_____
_____
_____
_____
_____
_____
_____

Directions continued:

Photos & Notes:

Recipe Name:
_____
_____

Date: _____

Type: _____

Difficulty: 1 2 3 4 5 6 7 8 9 10

Serves:
_____

Prep Time:
_____

Cook Time:
_____

Oven Temp:
_____

Notes:
_____
_____
_____
_____
_____

Ingredients:

_____
_____
_____
_____
_____
_____
_____
_____
_____
_____

Directions:

_____
_____
_____
_____
_____
_____
_____
_____
_____

Directions continued:

_____
_____
_____
_____
_____
_____
_____
_____
_____
_____
_____
_____

Photos & Notes:

Recipe Name:
_____
_____

Date: _____
Type: _____
Difficulty: 1 2 3 4 5 6 7 8 9 10

Serves:
_____

Prep Time:
_____

Cook Time:
_____

Oven Temp:
_____

Notes:
_____
_____
_____
_____
_____

Ingredients:

_____
_____
_____
_____
_____
_____
_____
_____
_____
_____
_____

Directions:

_____
_____
_____
_____
_____
_____
_____
_____
_____
_____

Directions continued:

_____
_____
_____
_____
_____
_____
_____
_____
_____
_____
_____
_____

Photos & Notes:

Recipe Name:
_____
_____

Date: _____
Type: _____
Difficulty: 1 2 3 4 5 6 7 8 9 10

Serves:
_____

Prep Time:
_____

Cook Time:
_____

Oven Temp:
_____

Notes:
_____
_____
_____
_____
_____

Ingredients:

Directions:

Directions continued:

_____
_____
_____
_____
_____
_____
_____
_____
_____
_____
_____
_____
_____

Photos & Notes:

Recipe Name:

_____

_____

Date: _____

Type: _____

Difficulty: 1 2 3 4 5 6 7 8 9 10

Serves:

_____

Prep Time:

_____

Cook Time:

_____

Oven Temp:

Notes:

_____

_____

_____

_____

_____

_____

Ingredients:

_____
_____
_____
_____
_____
_____
_____
_____
_____
_____

Directions:

_____
_____
_____
_____
_____
_____
_____
_____
_____

Directions continued:

Photos & Notes:

Recipe Name:

_____

_____

Date: _____

Type: _____

Difficulty: 1 2 3 4 5 6 7 8 9 10

Serves:

_____

Prep Time:

_____

Cook Time:

_____

Oven Temp:

_____

Notes:

_____

_____

_____

_____

_____

Ingredients:

_____
_____
_____
_____
_____
_____
_____
_____
_____
_____
_____
_____

Directions:

_____
_____
_____
_____
_____
_____
_____
_____
_____
_____
_____
_____
_____

Directions continued:

_____
_____
_____
_____
_____
_____
_____
_____
_____
_____
_____

Photos & Notes:

Recipe Name:
_____
_____

Date: _____
Type: _____
Difficulty: 1 2 3 4 5 6 7 8 9 10

Serves:
_____

Prep Time:
_____

Cook Time:
_____

Oven Temp:

Notes:
_____
_____
_____
_____
_____

Ingredients:
_____
_____
_____
_____
_____
_____
_____
_____
_____
_____
_____

Directions:
_____
_____
_____
_____
_____
_____
_____
_____
_____

Directions continued:

Photos & Notes:

Recipe Name:

_____

_____

Date: _____

Type: _____

Difficulty: 1 2 3 4 5 6 7 8 9 10

Serves:

_____

Prep Time:

_____

Cook Time:

_____

Oven Temp:

Notes:

_____

_____

_____

_____

_____

Ingredients:

_____

_____

_____

_____

_____

_____

_____

_____

_____

_____

_____

Directions:

_____

_____

_____

_____

_____

_____

_____

_____

_____

_____

Directions continued:

Photos & Notes:

Recipe Name:

_____
_____

Date: _____

Type: _____

Difficulty: 1 2 3 4 5 6 7 8 9 10

Serves:

_____

Prep Time:

_____

Cook Time:

_____

Oven Temp:

Notes:

_____
_____
_____
_____
_____
_____

Ingredients:

_____
_____
_____
_____
_____
_____
_____
_____
_____

Directions:

_____
_____
_____
_____
_____
_____
_____
_____
_____

Directions continued:

_____
_____
_____
_____
_____
_____
_____
_____
_____
_____
_____
_____

Photos & Notes:

Made in United States
North Haven, CT
12 October 2024

58774581R00061